PROPHECY
CHUR

Also available in the Pioneer *Perspectives* series:

The Role and Ministry of Women   Martin Scott

For further information on the Pioneer *Perspectives*
series and Pioneer, please write to:
P.O. Box 79c, Esher, Surrey, KT10 9LP

PROPHECY
IN THE
CHURCH

Martin Scott

PROPHECY IN THE CHURCH

ISBN   0-85009-726-6   (Australia ISBN 1-86258-194-0)

Unless otherwise indicated, Scripture quotations are from the HOLY BIBLE, NEW INTERNATIONAL VERSION (NIV). Copyright © 1973, 1978, 1984 by International Bible Society.

Front cover illustration: courtesy of "The Image Bank".

Reproduced, printed and bound in Great Britain for Word (UK) Ltd. by Clays Ltd., St Ives plc.

FOREWORD

Pioneer *Perspectives* are perhaps more than their title suggests!

They are carefully researched presentations of material, on important issues, appealing to thinking churches, creative leaders and responsible Christians.

Each *Perspective* pioneers in as much as it is at the cutting edge of biblical and theological issues. Each will continue to pioneer with new ideas, concepts and data drawn from Scripture, history and a contemporary understanding of both.

They are perspectives in as much as they aim to be an important contribution to the ongoing debate on issues such as women in ministry and leadership; prophets and prophecy in the church; biblical models of evangelism; integrating and discipling new believers; growing and building local churches and further perspectives on Christ's second coming.

Importantly, these studies use a journal style of presentation, and are written by people who are currently working out the implications of the issues they are writing about, in local churches. This is vital if we are to escape the dangerous fantasy of abstract theology without practical experience. They are not written to contribute to the paralysis of analysis—rather to feed, strengthen, nurture and inform so that we can be equipped to get God's will done, by networking the nations with the Gospel using all the resources that are available to us.

God's Word is always an event. How much we thank Him that He has left us an orderly account of what He wants us to believe, how He wants us to live, and what He wants us to do in order to bring heaven to the earth. As we embrace a better understanding of Scripture, rooted in local church, national and international mission, we shall become a part of the great eschatological purpose of bringing back the King—not for a church defeated, cowering and retiring but for one which, despite colossal odds, pressures and persecutions, is faithful to her Lord and His word. To do that we must 'search the Scriptures' to see if many of these 'new things' are true. I commend these *Perspectives* to you as they are published on a regular basis throughout these coming years.

Gerald Coates
Director Pioneer Trust/Team Leader

ACKNOWLEDGEMENTS

With thanks to all in Cobham—particularly to my wife Sue and good friend Steve Clifford and, finally, to two great children—Benjamin and Judith.

With respect to this particular subject I want to acknowledge and thank Dale Gentry for his input. It was he who first opened my eyes to the nature of the prophetic office.

The material presented has been gleaned from various sources over the years. It is possible some is original but I cannot claim with authority that this is the case. I want to express personal thanks to Gerald Coates who was one of the first people I saw prophesy in a non-religious fashion. He has also trusted me over the years and was a great help in starting me on the journey of discovering God's voice for others.

With regard to the editing of this volume I want to thank Chris Bourne who gave many hours to the hard work of making this book readable.

Martin Scott
July 1991

Pioneer consists of a team and network of churches, committed to dynamic and effective biblical Christianity.

The national team act as advisers and consultants to churches, which in many cases develop into a partnership with the Pioneer team. These are the churches keen to identify with the theology, philosophy, ethos and purpose of Pioneer. The team have a vigorous youth ministry, church-planting strategy and evangelistic emphasis.

Training courses include Equipped to Lead, Emerging Leaders and the highly successful TIE teams (Training In Evangelism).

Pioneer have also been instrumental in initiating and funding March for Jesus (with Ichthus/YWAM); Jubilee Campaign (for the suffering church worldwide); and ACET (Aids Care Education Training).

CONTENTS

PREFACE   11

CHAPTER 1 : An Introduction to Prophecy   13

CHAPTER 2 : Hearing God's Voice   19
  1. Believe in a speaking God   20
  2. Talk to God in everyday life   21
  3. Discover the voice of God   22
  4. Understand how prophecy comes   24

CHAPTER 3 : Getting Started   27
  1. Desire to prophesy (1 Cor. 14:1)   27
  2. Pray prophetically   28
  3. Speak in tongues in your private life   28
  4. Come under the spirit of prophecy   29
  5. Don't look for the hidden mystery   31
  6. Give what you have   32
  7. Prophesy according to your faith (Romans 12:6) 34

CHAPTER 4 : Guidelines to Giving Prophecy   35
  1. Personal not private words   36
  2. Give the prophecy to the right people   37
  3. Do not use prophecy to avoid confrontation 38
  4. Do not use prophecy to gain an identity   38
  5. Beware of the possibility of being enticed 39
  6. Do not be forced to go beyond your revelation 40
  7. Keep within the realm of prophecy   40

CHAPTER 5 : Guidelines to Receiving Prophecy   43
  1. Weigh it in spirit   43
  2. Realise a prophecy will be in part   45
  3. Realise a prophecy will fall into different 45
    categories
      i) a now word
      ii) a future word
      iii) a confirmatory word
      iv) new words

4. Record the word, meditate on it and pray   47
   over it (1 Timothy 1:18)
5. Open it up for fellowship and interpretation   48
6. Make preparation for it at the appropriate time   49

CHAPTER 6 : Prophets and Prophecy   51
1. Inspiration and revelation   52
2. A foundational ministry   54
3. Beyond the realm of prophecy   55
4. A divergence of ministry   55
5. Churches need to be committed to see   56
   prophets released

CHAPTER 7 : The Prophet and Other Ministries   59
1. Prophets together   59
2. Prophets and teachers   61
3. Prophets and apostles   61

CHAPTER 8 : Prophetic Ministry and Leadership   63

PREFACE

I was motivated to write this book because of a desire to see the gift of prophecy grow within the church. I have been very blessed, helped and inspired through personal words that have been prophesied to me over the years. At times those words have come at key times and have literally shaped whole phases of my life. I have also seen many lives touched and changed through prophetic words that God has been kind enough to allow me to bring.

Prophecy is a gift open to all. Yet it is a gift which can easily be misused resulting in damage. For this further reason I have wanted to put in print some guidelines which will help safeguard the use of prophecy. I often use the term 'prophet' in this book. I have not used it in order to denote that those who have been appointed to this office are only men. I use this term inclusive of all who exercise this ministry gift—male and female. I chose to use this generic term simply because it is much simpler than continually writing 'prophet or prophetess'.

Dale Gentry's example of the prophetic office has been a great stimulus to me. His teaching has been an influence on me and on this book. There are a number of areas—probably the two chapters on guidelines in particular—which have been greatly influenced directly and indirectly by his teaching. This is not to say that he nor anyone else has endorsed the contents of this book. For that I stand responsible.

CHAPTER 1

AN INTRODUCTION TO PROPHECY

This book is intended to serve as an introduction to the vast subject of prophecy. There will be large areas which will not be touched on—perhaps two of the most notable ones are the connection of music, worship and prophecy and the use of prophetic drama. Such related subjects are outside the scope of this book.

If some of the terms used in this book are unfamiliar to you then I suggest you read through Paul's teaching as found in 1 Corinthians chapters 12—14. In chapter 12 he outlines some manifestations or gifts of the Holy Spirit which are for the encouragement of the body of Christ. In chapter 13 he describes how these manifestations are to be used. Love is the key to seeing them used in a way which will benefit others. Love is not described as a superior gift—he calls it the superior way (1 Cor. 12:31). Then in chapter 14 he gives particular attention to the 'vocal gifts' of prophecy, speaking in tongues and the interpreting of those tongues.

I believe it is very helpful to see the gifts of the Holy Spirit as tools God gives us to fulfil a task in a specific situation. For this reason I prefer the term 'manifestations' of the Spirit to the term 'gifts' of the Spirit. The term 'gift' can give the impression of something which becomes our possession. I am not denying that there are ministry gifts which Christ calls individuals into; however, the 'spirituals'[1] which Paul lists in 1 Corinthians 12:7–11 are open for all to move in.

In 1 Corinthians 12:7 when Paul states that 'to each one

the manifestation of the Spirit is given' it might appear that these are gifts given to each individual as their possession. However, the context of this passage is of believers gathering together and the Holy Spirit being active. At such times the Holy Spirit moves and begins to manifest His presence. Such manifestations are through people of His choosing. On another occasion He might choose other people.

Again when consideration is given to the Greek tense Paul chooses here for the verb 'is given', I believe it points us to accepting that these are far more manifestations of the Spirit than some gift which is our possession. Paul uses the present tense which might be better translated 'is being given'. Had he meant that these were gifts which had been given to the individual and now they carried these gifts around with them, he could have shown this by choosing either one of two common Greek past tenses—either the aorist or perfect tense—which then would be translated as 'the manifestation of the Spirit has been given for the common good'.

To summarise, I maintain that these tools are basically situational and not residential. They are given to us when we need them. The Holy Spirit is residential in us and he can manifest Himself through us in different situations. What practical difference does this make? Simply this. In any given situation we can expect God to move through us. We don't need to wonder if God has given us a suitable gift but we can live realising that none of the gifts of the Spirit are out of bounds to us.

Obviously the Holy Spirit must give the inspiration but we are unlikely to move in any manifestation while there is no expectancy. If we are aware of the presence of the Holy Spirit and that He is longing to show His presence to be real, then I believe we will be more expectant of His moving. With regard to prophecy this simply means that we can all move in prophecy to one degree or another. It is not dependent on us being classed as 'prophets'.

This book will primarily be concerned with the gift of prophecy and also the ministry of the prophet. However, some brief definitions might be helpful before embarking on the main subject matter.

'Speaking in tongues' or 'glossalalia' as it is often known has become widespread ever since what is now known as the charismatic movement began around 1960 or so. 'Tongues' is simply an old English word for languages. In fact we still use this in the term 'mother tongue' today. So speaking in tongues simply means to speak in languages which have never been learned by the speaker. On the Day of Pentecost this supernatural event drew a large crowd (Acts 2:11). On that day the languages the disciples spoke in were actual languages spoken in the different nations who were represented in Jerusalem, by those who had gathered to celebrate the Jewish festival of Pentecost.

In 1 Corinthians 13:1 Paul speaks of there being languages of 'men and of angels'. We might paraphrase this as there being 'earthly and heavenly languages'. So a perscn who speaks in tongues will be speaking a language which they have never been taught. This will be a supernatural act inspired by the Holy Spirit and might be an earthly language, or indeed it might be a heavenly language.

It is the conviction of the writer that this is a gift which is open to all who have been immersed in the Holy Spirit. From Paul's teaching it is clear that there is a private use of the gift. Paul calls this 'praying with the spirit' (1 Cor. 14:15). Praying in this way will edify the person who is praying (1 Cor. 14:4). They will have an assurance that they will be praying effectively even if they do not understand what they are praying. Many times as well this simple, yet supernatural, gift will enable the speaker to worship God and express their love to Him, even when they feel that their native language has become inadequate to express that love.

Alongside this there is the public use of speaking in tongues. When a tongue is given publicly it will need to be interpreted so that those who have heard the tongue can also benefit from it. In Corinth it seems this was one of the areas Paul had to address in bringing some order back to their meetings. It seems that they often had people speaking out in tongues without any subsequent interpretation. This resulted in confusion. This and other similar areas of abuse probably account for Paul's instruction to limit the use of tongues to two or three per meeting. He gives corrective teaching, and it would not seem that this is a strict rule to be applied in every situation today.

The final manifestation of the Spirit which is covered in 1 Corinthians 14 is the gift of prophecy. This is the subject matter for this book. Prophecy is a large subject but a simple definition would be that the person who prophesies speaks forth on behalf of God. As they speak they declare the will and purpose of God.

Prophets and prophecy have always been the subject of controversy. By definition, when God speaks to individuals and nations it is to make His will and His thoughts clear. This is not always welcome and there will often be people who resent, fear or despise these divine interruptions. This is no less true today than it was in the times of the Old Testament. It is not easy to reach a clear understanding of prophecy, let alone discover how the gift should best be operated in the local church. That is why this book has been produced. This study is not designed to be exhaustive but simply to begin to open the subject up in a practical and biblical framework.

Throughout Scripture prophecy is regarded as a powerful and authoritative manifestation of the Holy Spirit. In the Old Testament prophesying is generally restricted to those who were called prophets. The place of prophecy in the New Testament is even greater than in the Old. The office of the prophet is maintained but the ability to prophesy is extended to include all those who are born of the Spirit.

Over the years some Christians have maintained that the gift of prophecy died out at the time when the first apostles died or, alternatively, when the canon of Scripture was completed. These two views not only contradict each other (over two hundred and fifty years separate the two events), they also fail to meet the conditions set in Scripture for the end of prophecy (and tongues and knowledge). The main passage to support such views of cessation is 1 Corinthians 13:8–13. The condition set upon the end of prophetic manifestation is that it will happen when we no longer need it. Whatever our interpretation of the phrase 'when perfection has come' we can not take it to refer to the Bible. The passage says that when the perfect has come we will no longer see things 'as a poor reflection' but we will see clearly. The perfect is said to come when we see 'face to face'.

The simple fact remains that we still see 'in a glass, darkly'. We still need our heavenly Father's encouragement, we still need to know His specific will in our circumstances. The church still needs to hear the voice of her God, perhaps today more than ever. Prophecy is not dead, and for the last two thousand years there have always been groups of Christians who knew this and often knew the persecution of the religious authorities in the process! Those who hold that prophecy is dead have to create some very strange explanations for why it is still alive. Part of the problem has been situated in the idea of prophecy as a mystical gift which people 'have' rather than as an expression of the life of the Holy Spirit. Prophecy happens because God is a person who speaks. It is simply one of the things that the Holy Spirit does when He is free to do as He wishes.

Prophecy, then, should be a normal part of church life although it is not to become a substitute for Scripture, prayer or godly counsel. It is another means by which God speaks. It is one of the ways in which He enables us, individually and corporately, to maintain a life which is centred in Him. Prophecy is a gift which we should expect to be poured out liberally during the age of the Holy Spirit (Joel 2:28–32; Acts 2:17,18). So much so that Paul stated 'you can all prophesy in turn' (1 Cor. 14:31) and encouraged us to desire eagerly the gift of prophecy (1 Cor. 14:1).

Prophecy is a gift which can radically change the course of a person's life or even that of a nation—it is to be held in honour. There are however some guidelines which will ensure that the gift is not misused and does not cause damage or confusion. The guidelines outlined in later chapters of this book are biblically based and practical. They stem from the outworking of the prophetic gift within the local church. These guidelines should ensure that prophecy genuinely edifies and strengthens the body of Christ. Without guidelines prophecy can become dangerous. If it is not understood it can easily be abused. However the answer to misuse is not disuse but correct use. The guidelines of Scripture and experience both serve to keep the gift pure and our walk straight.

---

1. There is no word 'gifts' in the original Greek of 1 Corinthians 12:1. Paul simply speaks of the 'spirituals'.

CHAPTER 2

HEARING GOD'S VOICE

Prophecy is a powerful tool that God has given to the church. Through prophecy we can actually listen to the living God speak to us today. God loves to communicate to us His love, His care and His knowledge. He can do this in many ways but He often chooses to do so through prophecy.

Jesus was known as 'a prophet powerful in word and deed' (Luke 24:19) and spoke supernaturally to people on a number of different occasions. He spoke to Nathanael, revealing his heart and even where he was when Philip spoke to him (John 1:43–51). This immediately brought a response of faith from him. In John chapter 4 we find Jesus in conversation with a woman at a well in Samaria. She left convinced that here was someone who knew everything she had ever done (John 4:39). It was through prophecy and the related gift of the word of knowledge that He revealed these facts on these and other occasions.

We might never have testimonies quite as spectacular as those few which we have quoted from the life of Jesus, but as we begin to move out in prophecy I am sure God will communicate so much of Himself to others through us. In our own church numerous people have been challenged and transformed, as they have responded to personal words of prophecy which spoke into the very depths of their own spirits.

Through prophecy, teams have been given details of what will take place on their ministry trips. They have been warned of difficult situations ahead—of areas where the enemy was seeking to trap them. In those situations they were thankful that they were not, to quote the apostle Paul, unaware of the schemes of the enemy (2 Cor. 2:11). At other times teams have known who to invest in because they have received a description of that person through a prophetic word beforehand.

Prophecy has proved invaluable. On one occasion a visiting speaker was informed through prophecy that in three months' time he would be used in a sign and a wonder. That was the entire content of the prophecy. He duly noted in his diary that the date prophesied would be at the end of his holiday. He really did not know what this could mean, but to the best of his ability he made himself available to God and sure enough, right at the end of his holiday he had to rush back because the daughter of one of his co-elders had been rushed into hospital. She was subsequently moved from that hospital in Sussex to one of the larger hospitals in the London area—complete with police escort. Due to her condition she had to be moved very slowly with all the necessary roads closed off to normal traffic. Few people survive her condition and those who do normally are left with lasting effects. They visited the hospital and God's word was fulfilled. I often wonder whether this leader would have been ready, had God not warned him in advance through that prophetic word.

Examples of this nature could be repeated many times over from numerous churches. I believe that this will increase as the church sees a full restoration of the various manifestations of the Holy Spirit.

There are two important questions that we all ask when prophecy is discussed. How do we hear God speak and how do we know that it is really God who has spoken? There is probably no easy foolproof answer but I want to put forward some suggestions in the remainder of this chapter. The chapter which follows will also help in this respect.

1. Believe in a speaking God

The Bible reveals that God is a God who speaks. The first book of the Old Testament does not argue for the existence of God—it boldly states that God exists and that He speaks

(Gen.1:1–3). The writer of the book of Hebrews picks this up with the words 'God spoke . . . at many times and in various ways' (Heb. 1:1). It seems that the conviction of the Bible writers was that God speaks. Speech might even be described as one of the most fundamental activities of God.

If I believe that God is there and He is not silent then I can begin to expect that He will speak to me—and maybe even that He might speak through me!

Once we discover that speaking is in the very nature of God we can raise our expectations of hearing from Him. This is the first step to hearing the voice of God because God responds to expectancy and faith.

2. Talk to God in everyday life

Prayer is not some religious duty we are to be involved in—it is simply the believer talking to God. Even with those of us who regularly talk to God, we often fall into the trap of not talking to Him other than when we are in 'request mode'. We should try and develop a lifestyle where we regularly talk to Him about everything, regardless of where we are. By so doing I believe we will be opening the channel of communication from us to Him—and vice versa. It should then be no surprise when He catches us unawares and speaks to us—sometimes seemingly about the most mundane of things. God loves doing that. Perhaps it might be as simple as God speaking to us while we are out walking, appreciating the different colours that He has placed in this world. At such times God can draw along side, and before we realise it we find ourselves meditating on the endless variety there is within creation. Our thoughts might move on as we consider that God is always doing something new, and that is why the church is experiencing new things.

It might not be profound but we have heard God speak. Through it we will come to a deeper understanding of what He is doing and, very importantly, we will be getting our ear attuned to His voice.

3. Discover the voice of God

I am sure that many people—and not just Christians—
hear the voice of God but do not recognise it. Sometimes it
will come as a result of having a great concern. Perhaps it
might come as we watch the news and become burdened
over something. Often this occurs but once the news is
over we switch off and forget it. These are often occasions
when God is speaking to us but we fail to hear His voice.

This can be how God will get our attention to speak out
a prophecy. We might receive a growing conviction about
something and as we wait expectantly, clarity comes to the
burden so it can be expressed verbally. The only word of
warning I would like to offer here is that we need to discern
when God is speaking to us about ourselves, and when He
is speaking to us for others. We must not try and project the
voice of God to us about ourselves on to others, by claiming
that God is speaking to them.

God obviously speaks to us through the Bible. I expect
we have all had the experience of reading some verses and
all of a sudden they seem to jump out of the page at us. It
is as if we have never ever read them before. That experience
really is God speaking directly to us. It can also happen
through reading a book other than the Bible—I have even
experienced it while watching television.

God wants to speak. I remember the time He spoke to
me and put something prophetic in my spirit through a
phrase I heard on the television. I was getting ready to go
out to one of our regular meetings; my mind not being on
anything in particular, I aimlessly turned on the television.
An advert was on and I caught the closing line which was
'the future belongs to those who prepare for it'. It was as if
a light was turned on for me and I knew immediately that
this was actually a prophetic word for the church. These
experiences will help us to recognise the Lord's voice.

God can speak through coincidences that occur or simply
through very natural occurrences. There are a number of
examples of this in the Bible. Perhaps the best known is
when Jeremiah went to the potter's shed and saw the
potter make a pot, only to discover a flaw in it. He had to

break it and start all over again. As Jeremiah saw this he realised that this was God's word to Israel—God had found a flaw in them and He was breaking them, but only so that He could remould them (Jer.18:1-10). Something natural became the means by which Jeremiah heard the voice of God.

Another example from the Bible is of Samuel and Saul. In 1 Samuel chapter 15 Saul is rebuked by Samuel, who then turns to leave. Saul is distressed and pleads that Samuel stay. In desperation he grabs hold of Samuel's cloak which inevitably tears. Instantly Samuel realises that this illustrates the word of the Lord to Saul. He proclaims, 'The Lord has torn the kingdom of Israel from you today and has given it to one of your neighbours—to one better than you' (1 Sam. 15:28). The natural event became the catalyst for Samuel to hear the voice of God.

If we ask God to anoint our ears and our eyes, then many times we will hear and see things which will become the catalyst for us to hear God speak. From some very ordinary and natural events God can put something in our spirits which will be truly prophetic. If we allow God to take the initiative and we respond, then it will surprise us how often God can speak through this.

For a number of years I have taken a workshop session during the summer months on prophecy for teams who are being trained in evangelism. On many different occasions I have picked someone out of the workshop who is wearing something colourful, often a T-shirt, and many times one with a picture on it. I then ask people to describe what they see with their natural eyes, and follow it up by showing them the parallel of what they are naturally looking at and what has been taking place in this person's life spiritually. It amazes them (and myself) how easy God makes it. The right person is always wearing the right piece of clothing! Provided we don't try to force it to happen God will help us to communicate His word to others. Remember God loves to speak and He wants to help us to hear His voice.

In all of this it is important that our motivation is right.

We are not to be motivated by looking good or impressing others. The only true and safe motivation is a desire to love people and see God make Himself real to them.

Another very important key to hear God speak is to spend time waiting on Him. It is recorded that God spoke a most profound word to a group of prophets and teachers as they met together at Antioch. The word released a whole mission to the Gentile world. It is interesting to note that Luke did not say that they met together with the express purpose of hearing from God, but he states that God spoke 'while they were worshipping the Lord and fasting' (Acts 13:1–3). They wanted to spend time in His presence and it was into that context that God spoke and they recognised His voice. If we spend time with God for no other reason than that we love Him, we will soon begin to discover His voice—we will recognise His voice because we will know Him.

4. Understand how prophecy comes

The Hebrew word for 'prophet' is the word *nabi*. It is derived from a root word meaning to well up, to spring forth, to bubble up. It is reminiscent of Jesus' words when He described the Holy Spirit becoming like streams of living water flowing from within a person (John 7:37–39). Prophecy does not normally come from outside us—it is rather something which will come from within and begin to 'bubble forth'. Sometimes we are waiting to hear from God, almost imagining it will come from outer space. God however wants us to get started by giving the little bit we have, and as we do that more will 'bubble up'. Sometimes all we might have is a few words or thoughts. We cannot determine how much insight we have but as we give the little amount we feel we have, we will make room for more to bubble up to the surface.

Learning to hear the voice of God is an exciting path that He wants us to embark on. When it comes to prophesying it is important to know that we are not making it all up. A very good safeguard is to ask the question 'Is this the sort of thing Jesus would be saying if He were here now?' If we begin to prophesy God's word to people, we need to be asking to feel a little of what God feels for this particular situation. If we take this approach we will not go far wrong.

Alongside all of this we need to discover friends around us who are ready to encourage and correct us. If we can operate in an environment of acceptance and approval it will help us relax and reach out to God with real care.

This chapter has probably not answered all of your questions about hearing the voice of God, but I believe it should put you on the right course. The next chapter picks up a similar theme and I am sure that between these two chapters good foundations will be laid in your own experience for you to hear God for yourself and for others.

CHAPTER 3

GETTING STARTED

To many people prophecy and the gifts of the Holy Spirit are a mystery. Paul stated that he did not want us ignorant concerning the 'spirituals' (1 Cor. 12:1). It is clear that although the manifestations of the Holy Spirit are supernatural they are not to be 'spooky' nor mysterious. For many the problem is one of practice rather than of principle. They simply don't know how to get started, or even if they are allowed to try. Consequently the prophetic realm remains as a mystery to them. If one of the hallmarks of the age of the Holy Spirit is prophecy, then it is certain that God wants to clear away the confusion so that we can begin to experience and benefit from the prophetic gifts.

Listed below are a number of points which will help you begin to be active in prophecy; or at least prepare your life for God to be able to speak through you.

1. Desire to prophesy (1 Cor. 14:1)

There is one simple rule—you will never prophesy if you don't want to! The manifestations of the Holy Spirit are powerful but they are not generally compulsive. We need to begin by having a desire to be used by God in prophecy. This desire is not to boost our image or prove our status; it is to edify, encourage and comfort the church of Jesus. If our desire to prophesy is to bless and love people then we are seeking God for the right reasons—if not then we need to stop and allow God to sort out our motives. For this reason we would expect to find that a person who is developing in a prophetic gift is also developing a growing care for people, which is being expressed both practically and in prayer.

When we begin to prophesy we should not try to see ourselves as prophets or even as someone who has a prophetic ministry. The ministry or office of the prophet is quite distinct from the more general gift of prophesying. A heavy concern with the image or calling of the prophet can become an obsession, potentially leading us into fantasy and even deception. We must start simply by seeking to bless others and by praying to God that He will give us the tools necessary to fulfil that desire—one of which is prophecy.

2. Pray prophetically

There is one doorway for prophetic action which is always open to us. Prayer is a hallmark of the people who prophesy. When we pray we need to learn to recognise God's voice so that He can direct our prayers. Prophetic praying is not a monologue nor the presentation of a shopping list—it is discovering the will of God in a situation and then praying 'your will be done'. If we begin to be 'moved by the burden of the Lord' or, in other words, to feel His concerns and to share His desires, then we will be beginning to learn how to prophesy.

This applies whether we are praying for a situation or an individual. As we pray we will sense that we should concentrate on some specific point. On many occasions we will discover later that this was, in fact, direction that God was giving us. The same is true with individuals—if we will begin to thank God for them and allow the Holy Spirit to move us, we will find ourselves praying for them in the very area of their need. This can be the first step to moving into the prophetic realm.

3. Speak in tongues in your private life

This particular area is difficult to overemphasise. Tongues might be the least of the gifts, but it is a very precious gift which enables us to communicate with God in a most unique and supernatural way. Our modern minds tend to devalue anything we do not understand. The gift of tongues is a real prayer language; we might not fully understand what the Holy Spirit is saying but we can be absolutely certain the prayer in tongues is made precisely according to God's will. Speaking in tongues is not to be reserved for our meetings together nor even for our private devotions—it is a gift freely given, for use at all times and in all situations.

If we regularly speak in tongues to God then our own spirits will be edified. We will be strengthened and built up, and we have a greater 'reservoir' from which to release God's love and blessing. To speak in tongues is to flow in a manifestation of the Holy Spirit. As we develop the habit of frequently and regularly speaking to God in the language He gives us, so we will find it much easier to flow in prophecy—which is simply another manifestation of the Holy Spirit.

4. Come under the spirit of prophecy

In our church meetings there will be times when the Holy Spirit manifests Himself in such a way that there is a liberal release of prophetic words. The Holy Spirit inspires one prophetic word to follow another. We could term this a release of 'the spirit of prophecy'. At such times even those who do not regularly prophesy will find that they can do so.

A biblical example of this is found in 1 Samuel 10:9–13. Saul was about to enter the city of Gibeah when he met a company of prophets. As a result of being in their company Saul too began to prophesy. This led to the question, 'Is Saul also among the prophets?' Saul was not a prophet but he came under the 'spirit of prophecy' at this point and so began to prophesy.

When such a release of the prophetic gifts happens in a meeting, the best response is to allow your spirit to move with the prophetic spirit. Prophecy is a result of being moved by the Holy Spirit (or 'carried along' by the Holy Spirit as in 2 Peter 1:21). As we respond to the moving of the Holy Spirit we will be taught what it is like to be moved prophetically. This will be a great help to us in discerning between a simple emotional feeling and the movement of the Holy Spirit.

Incidentally this is the only true means of discerning prophetic words which are given. Much that passes for discernment of a prophecy is little more than deciding whether or not we agree with what has been said! Prophecy is not discerned by the mind but by the spirit. While a prophetic word is being given we should be open to God, not sitting in silent judgement, which is often simply a 'spiritualised' form of cynicism. We should allow the Holy Spirit to move us in the direction of the word—if we find that it is not possible to 'go' with the word, then normally it is safe to assume that there is a problem with the word. We have discerned that prophecy in our spirit. Obviously we need to grow in maturity in order to discern accurately, but this has to be the starting point with regard to discernment.

You might be puzzled as to why the mind is of little use in discerning the genuineness of a prophecy. All that the mind can do is to decide if the prophecy agrees with Scripture (as far as we know it) or if we agree with it ourselves, which is hardly the point. We can, of course, be sure that any word which actively opposes the Bible is not of God. But if we try to discern prophecy by the mind, then we will tend to accept anything which is in accord with the teaching of Scripture, which does automatically make it prophetic. In short, the reason for judging prophecy is not to see if it is biblically sound, but to see if this is what God is actually saying to us. We must follow prophecy with a response of faith and obedience and we must not give our obedience lightly to every word and idea simply because it is spoken in a certain way.

Again there are times that God speaks and our minds are actually offended. If we discern the word simply by our minds we might many times reject the word outright. However, there are times God comes to offend our minds in order to get our attention and to reach deep into our spirits. So we do not lay on one side our critical faculties, but the real area where we discern is not the mind but the spirit.

So the correct response when prophetic words begin to come is to 'go with the flow'. In so doing many times God begins to give further revelation to those who are listening. It seems that those listening can gain a momentum from the previous words and as a result are able to follow on from those words. This seems to be the situation Paul describes in 1 Corinthians 14:29–33. There he says that a further revelation might well come to those listening while there is prophecy going on—at which point the one with the further revelation needs to carry on. This will only occur where those listening are actively seeking to respond and interact with the prophetic words. They are not simply listening but are actively interacting with the words which are being spoken.

5. Don't look for the hidden mystery

It is often assumed that to be prophetic we must reveal some hidden thing or bring a message that no one has ever heard before. However, prophecy is rarely mysterious or even particularly radical. It is not how profound or 'deep' the word is that makes it prophetic—it is the combination of the person or situation and the word given that makes it prophetic. The simplest of words given to the right situation at the right time can have a profound impact. It is the difference between saying that something is God's word because it is in the Bible, and being sure that this is what God is saying to that person right now. In this sense prophecy allows people to own and trust what God says in a new way, so that it becomes dynamic truth in their life. So we should not look for the word which we think will impress or startle people. We must allow God to make the impact; our concern is that the words we bring should be for 'strengthening, encouragement and comfort'.

We should also be very careful about trying to give too

many details, particularly in the early stages of developing a prophetic gift . This applies to areas such as the giving of dates, places, names, etc. God can lead into this if He chooses but it is not advisable to begin with those areas of specifics. Prophecy is not speculation; it is not a guess which becomes authoritative because it is spoken in God's name. It is not uncommon for someone's early prophecies to be discerned as a mixture of inspiration and imagination (or desperation!). Mature leaders will often be able to mark the exact point at which revelation ended and the commentary began. Better by far that we should be faithful to exactly what God is saying.

6. Give what you have

We can be tempted to add to what God gives us so that we will look better. By adding to prophecy we can undermine and confuse the actual word that God wants given. Conversely we should not subtract from the prophetic word and leave areas out—unless we have clear instruction from the Lord not to release all of the word. This will not usually happen in the early days of prophesying—it requires a great clarity and a high level of confidence in the gift.

A friend of the writer was once struggling with a situation which seemed interminable. A few moments after crying inwardly 'How long Oh Lord!' they received a clear encouragement from the Lord through prophecy. The person simply spoke three words—'It will end.' It takes a brave person to give just three little words face to face—but what a difference they made coming from someone who knew nothing of the problem.

In another situation I was due to speak in a church. As the meeting progressed a young man walked in, and as he did so these words came vividly to my mind—tell that young man that what happened to his mother won't happen to him. While I was speaking I can recall trying to work out what it might have been that had happened to his mother—the truth was that I wanted to give a longer prophetic word than simply the above sentence. However, when I came to speak to the young man I had to be honest and simply go with the few words that had come to me. The response was immediate—he broke down and began to sob. I discovered later that his mother had recently died from a disease which the doctors had said was hereditary. I was so glad that I had not given in to the temptation to add to God's word. The young man had a burning question which God answered with an economy of words.

We do not know the full impact our words will have on a person. The words in themselves might not be profound—but our few words married to the specific situation can have the most profound results.

If we are convinced that we have a word from God, and that we also have some clear thoughts regarding the word but we are not so convinced that the thoughts are also from God, then we should make this clear as we deliver the prophecy. For example, if we felt clear that God is going to bless a certain group then we could say so with confidence. We might also think that the area of blessing will be by the end of the year and among young people. We can prophesy with confidence about the blessing of God, but then we would either need to share our thoughts privately afterwards, with those in responsibility, or at least preface it with 'and I think this is likely to be . . .' so that we are not giving the thoughts the same weight as the word which God has given to us.

The simple rule with prophecy is give it as we get it — don't pad it out with speculation or seek to balance the word.

A final comment is probably appropriate at this point on the language that we should use when we give a prophecy. Many times in the Bible prophets spoke and prefaced their words with a statement such as 'This is what God is saying'. However, not all the prophets spoke in this way and many times it is probably best not to use such terminology. It is often more appropriate to speak in a very straight forward way and preface it with a statement such as 'I believe God wants to say to us . . .' Again it is our choice whether we give a prophecy in the third person—'God would say to us. . .'or give it in the first person and speak on God's behalf directly—I say to you . . .'

In all of this we are simply to find the best means that will communicate the burden which God has given us. We are certainly not to try to appear religious or even spiritual. We are to be natural and allow God to be supernatural.

7. Prophesy according to your faith (Rom. 12:6)

This is a very clear limitation put on prophecy. We would not expect a beginner in prophecy to be prophesying revival of enormous scale, as that would be well beyond their faith level. In prophesying we need to be asking ourselves such questions as 'Can I really see this happening?' If we cannot then we need to ask whether God has spoken or not. Prophecy should cause faith to rise in the recipient but it should also cause a similar response in the person prophesying, because faith comes when we hear God speak (Rom. 10:17).

If we are to follow the points as outlined above then I do believe we will soon begin to move in prophecy with the right motivation. In the next chapter I want to give some guidelines, regarding the giving of prophetic words. These are guidelines, not a set of legalistic rules to be followed. However, it is important that we know how to administer the words that God gives us. There need to be checks and balances. This will enhance prophecy through protecting the gift, and will also ensure that the people to whom we give prophetic words are blessed and not damaged in any way.

CHAPTER 4

GUIDELINES TO GIVING PROPHECY

Prophecy is a gift of the Holy Spirit and comes through His inspiration. When someone prophesies, it might be assumed the Holy Spirit will ensure that the prophecy is given in the most fitting way. This is not the case. Paul says that the person prophesying has a great responsibility to ensure that everything is done in the most suitable way. He asks for order (1 Cor. 14:40—note it is *our* responsibility, not the Holy Spirit's). And specifically in the context of prophecy he states that the 'spirits of the prophets are subject to the control of the prophets' (1 Cor. 14:32).

Paul himself gives guidelines regarding the use of certain gifts in 1 Corinthians 14. These gifts of the Spirit can bring tremendous encouragement and blessing when handled correctly. However when mishandled they can cause considerable damage. For this reason this chapter is devoted to laying down certain guidelines to giving prophecy.

These guidelines are not a list of rules. In fact if a search is made of Scripture it is possible to find certain situations where some of these guidelines were not adhered to. However, the guidelines laid out here are both practical and biblically based. If someone continually disregarded these or similar guidelines I believe that they would be in grave danger of going against the spirit of Scripture. Before too long I am sure that their 'prophecies' would be causing trouble.

We are encouraged to test everything and hold on to what is good (1 Thess. 5:21). Paul gave this instruction in the context of responding to prophecies. If we are to take this seriously then I believe we need to establish sensible guidelines.

These guidelines will enable the right people to weigh what has been prophesied. They will also mean that those who prophesy can be helped in their delivery and content. Both those who receive and those who give prophecies should benefit.

Prophecy is to be spoken out and then it is to be weighed by those who are mature (1 Cor. 14:29; Heb. 5:11–14). Anyone who prophesies and is not prepared to have their words weighed, and consequently be open for personal correction, should not be allowed to prophesy—regardless of how mature their gift appears. There is no one who is beyond the need of accountability, and it is important that we do not end up compromising our position through intimidation. Even if someone appears to have a most remarkable gift, Scripture still insists that such a person must have a submissive heart. It might even be argued that the more gifted a person is the greater the need there is for accountability.

So below are certain guidelines which will enable all who prophesy to find an appropriate accountability.

1. Personal not private words

I do believe that God gives personal words to people. These words are to encourage and be a means of helping them fulfil the call of God on their lives. The area which needs to be guarded against is that of private prophecy. Private prophecy differs from personal prophecy. Private prophecy is where in a one-to-one situation there is no one to hear, weigh and help interpret the word.

There is nothing intrinsically wrong with private prophecy. The problem that arises is the absence of those who can bring objective discernment to the prophecy. This is not simply resolved by having more than one person involved when a word is given—it is having the right people involved. It is ideal for those who are pastorally responsible for that person to have access to the prophecy.

Certainly those who have the maturity to judge the word given need to be involved.

Private prophecy is open to much abuse for a number of reasons. The main area of abuse is that it can lead to some form of manipulation by the person prophesying. When no one is present to bring discernment it is easy to bring in elements, through vested interest or even through personal perspective, which are unhelpful and confusing. This can even happen when there has been no conscious desire to do so. There is also the danger of the person being prophesied over of being 'hooked up' to the other person in a totally unhelpful way. This can happen through a level of inordinate respect or conversely through something akin to manipulation. In other words the problem can be in the person giving the word or in the person receiving the word.

Along similar lines it is also very unwise and dangerous for someone to continue to look to a specific individual to give them prophetic words. It is one of the quickest and most certain ways of ending up in deception. God wants us to have specific relationships but he does not want us to become dependent on others in a way which is unhelpful.

Prophecy is to serve the overseers of a church and needs to be effectively weighed by those people. For this reason any delivery of prophecy which excludes overseers gaining access to the words spoken, and also to the speaker of those words, is dangerous and out of order. For these reasons private prophecy is dangerous and to be avoided.

2. Give the prophecy to the right people

Prophetic words are to be given to the right people. If a word is for someone in particular, then we would normally simply give it to the person concerned in a suitable context. However, on occasion it might not be best simply to give it directly to the person concerned. In such cases it needs to be submitted to leadership who can help give guidance as to what to do with the word. This would be particularly true if the prophecy contained elements of direction or correction. Sometimes all that needs adjusting is the time or the setting in which the word needs to be given, which again leadership can advise on.

In a meeting context it is also proper procedure to check a word out with the person leading the meeting so that they can discern if it is right to give the word or even if this is the right time. In all of this procedure the issue is simply of the speaker being accountable and open to correction.

3. Do not use prophecy to avoid confrontation

Matthew 18:15–17, along with other Scriptures, give us clear guidelines on how to maintain good healthy relationships. We are to speak the truth to one another in a spirit of love and reasonableness. If issues come between us we are to seek to resolve any differences face to face. If we cannot do so then Jesus outlines a very clear and effective procedure in the Matthew passage listed above.

At other times it is not simply that there is something between us, but that there are certain perspectives we have on someone—their attitudes or behaviour. In those situations we are not to use the cover of the prophetic to avoid personal confrontation. It is wrong at those times to use the prophetic approach of 'the Lord would say to you . . .' (Please also remember we can even adopt that approach without using such words.) We need to be real and acknowledge the need to sit down with the person concerned and speak honestly, humbly and with vulnerability.

4. Do not use prophecy to gain an identity

Many people who lack a sense of identity seek to gain identity through function and gift. A very common sphere for this is the prophetic arena. If pursued this will lead to fantasy in the early steps, and even the opening up to a spirit of false prophecy in the later steps. This is avoided by continuing to make your life available for comment by others—something which we never grow out of.

If someone refuses to come under God's legitimate and delegated authority, they will inevitably come under an illegitimate authority. Into this rebellious situation spirits of false prophecy are quick to move. Rebellion is akin to witchcraft (1 Sam. 15:23). Witchcraft is all about controlling others and if the rebellious person continues to prophesy they will seek to control or manipulate others through their prophecies.

All of this is simply avoided by making our lives accountable to others and continually seeking to find our identity in our relationship with God as our Father.

5. Beware of the possibility of being enticed

In prophecy there are a number of dangers that can arise where we are moved by something other than hearing God and the clear prompting of the Holy Spirit. Ezekiel 14:9 is a salutary warning to all who prophesy. In that passage God explains that He is set against the house of Israel at that time. In such a situation He brings a warning to the prophets who might be enticed to give a comforting word to those people who came seeking a word. Even then by implication it seems that if the prophet is enticed, God will allow a word to be given which is simply in line with the person's desires. This of course will not be a true word from the Lord, but will simply confirm the person in the path they are on.

So if prophets can be enticed to release words which people are wanting to hear, then all who prophesy need to take note. In such situations both the person giving and receiving the word are held accountable.

How do such things occur? I believe it can happen through a number of different possibilities. For example, it can happen where the one who prophesies is drawn out through strong sympathy for the person. They would like God to give this person a prophecy and are motivated at that level.

It is also possible to be enticed to give a word to a person who has prayed in agreement with someone else that they will receive a word—often this is where the people concerned have had an involvement in the occult and deceptive or seductive spirits are still at work.

I believe it is easy to avoid this area by asking God to bind such influences from us and then disciplining ourselves to move only in response to clear instruction from God. Refuse to be drawn through sympathy, strong desire, guilt, manipulation or any such thing. Again this highlights the need for accountability in these areas.

6. Do not be forced to go beyond your revelation

Many times after receiving a prophetic word the individuals want to discuss it. People need to be free to do this so anything can be clarified which has not been understood. However, if we allow ourselves to be drawn out to bring an explanation to the word we have brought, many times we simply end up bringing confusion.

Prophecy has at its heart revelation which comes from God. Many times this revelation needs to be interpreted, and further, the interpretation often needs to be applied. Sometimes the words given can be completely accurate and then mistakes are made over the interpretation or application of the words.

The revelation can be of God, but the other areas can be wrong if we feel forced to give an answer which we are not equipped and gifted to give. This can in turn discredit the prophetic word and could lead a person to follow a path that God did not mark out for the person.

The responsibility of the person prophesying is to give the revelation as God gave it to them. It might not be their responsibility to interpret any areas which need further explanation. Again this highlights the need for fellowship and accountability.

7. Keep within the realm of prophecy

Prophecy is to edify, exhort and to comfort (1 Cor. 14:3).

This is the normal realm for prophecy and most people have a great need of edification, exhortation and comfort. Alongside prophecy as a gift (which is open to all) there is the ministry of the prophet. A prophet can and often does go beyond the realm of prophecy as outlined by Paul in this Scripture. A prophet often deals with foundation and directional issues.

If we are moving under the gift of prophecy, we should stay within the guidelines given by Paul and not seek to emulate the ministry of the prophet. At a later stage it might become clear that we should be recognised and released into that by leadership. There would of course be a proven track record to back up this recognition.

An area where mistakes can be made is over the prophesying of future events. Other areas include that of giving specific dates and geographies. These are not areas for the beginner to move in, although many times God will cause a more mature ministry to move in these.

I believe there are certain areas which should be avoided—for instance prophesying who a person will get married to; prophesying the 'rightness' of people who are going out together. Finally, other areas where great care should be exercised are that of prophesying the gender of babies while in the womb (it is easier to prophesy that once they are born!) and of prophesying the ministry gifts over people.

As stated at the beginning of this chapter these guidlines are not a set of rules. However, I do believe it would be very rare for a person prophesying to go against any of the principles laid out above. The key issue, as has been continually stated, is that of accountability and fellowship.

In the next chapter we will look at prophecy from the recipient's point of view. We will seek to give certain guidelines that will help us as we seek to respond to God and His word. Prophecy can become a powerful tool to help us fulfil the call of God on our lives if handled correctly.

CHAPTER 5

GUIDELINES TO RECEIVING PROPHECY

Prophecy can be a tremendous tool to bring blessing and encouragement. In my own life certain specific prophecies have been invaluable in helping me to discern the will of God. For example, prophecies I have received outlining areas of ministry where God wanted to use me have been very helpful in responding to specific invitations for ministry. It is a great stimulus to faith to know that a particular engagement is one which fits within a specific area where God has promised to bless.

In the previous chapter I tried to give some clear, practical guidelines which will help to ensure that prophecy can be effectively weighed and judged. In this chapter I want to give some guidelines which will help us to receive the prophetic word and see that word fulfilled.

1. Weigh it in spirit

Scripture encourages us to discern prophecy. To discern prophecy is to judge it regarding its source as well as its content. A word which is often used to describe this process is the word 'weigh'. I believe this is a very descriptive word. In weighing it we are simply asking 'how does this measure up?'

The first area where we weigh prophecy is in discerning the 'spirit' of such a word. If a prophecy is accurate it does not necessarily mean that it is therefore from God. If this was the only criterion which we applied, I believe we would be in danger of eventually opening ourselves up to something deceptive. By following this pattern of discernment we could be opening up our lives to more than simply the prophetic word. We do need to weigh the accuracy of prophetic words, as accuracy is important but it is not everything. We can see this by Paul's reaction to some very accurate words spoken about himself and Silas while in Philippi. The words were true but the source from which the woman spoke was not God. (See Acts 16:16-18 for this story.)

Even if the prophecy contained certain inaccuracies we might still be able to receive the 'spirit' of the prophecy. This is not to excuse the person prophesying, but it is simply to underline that prophecy communicates more than simple facts. By adopting this approach we would first ask questions regarding the source of the spirit of the prophecy. This would include questions over what is being said, and finally we would consider the accuracy of what was said.

At this point we recall the earlier comments on discernment, where we outlined that prophecy is not discerned by the mind but is discerned spiritually. If a prophecy agrees with Scripture then that does not automatically make it a true prophetic word. Obviously if it clearly goes against the teaching and spirit of the Scriptures, then it is not a word from God. God does not contradict Himself —even if there are at times apparent paradoxes in what He says.

Also if it offends our mind and cuts across the way we think or our preconceptions, then this does not automatically mean that it is a false word. Sometimes it would even appear that God offends our minds so that He can gain our attention.

When weighing a word we need to know that it is perfectly in order to put a word on the 'shelf' until we receive further clarity regarding it. It is wrong and foolish to receive everything which is given in the name of the Lord. There will be times when we are unable to decide fully over a particular prophecy, and our response needs to be one of asking God for further clarification.

A general principle by which to operate is to only 'bin' a prophecy if it is clearly wrong. Otherwise we can keep a prophecy we are unsure of on file as clarity might come at a later date. This clarity might lead us either to accept or reject it at a later stage.

2. Realise a prophecy will be in part

In 1 Corinthians 13:9 Paul states that 'we prophesy in part'. When a prophecy is given it will not contain the whole counsel of God. If a personal prophecy is given to an individual it will not speak of everything concerning that person's life. If it did then it would discourage that individual from seeking God for themselves. Prophecy never discourages this—in fact prophecy is intended to produce the opposite effect. Prophecy will lead an individual to seek God even more.

If a prophecy is silent over certain areas this does not mean that God has nothing to say on the subject. And if a new prophecy does not mention certain elements which featured in previous prophecies, we should not immediately assume that either the new prophecy or the previous ones must therefore be wrong. The new word does not render all previous words null and void! In such situations the new word is simply adding to previous words. It should become a further help to us in discerning and subsequently fulfilling the purposes of God for our life.

Many times there is an economy of words from God and we need to allow Him to speak about the 'part' which is of concern to Him at this time.

3. Realise a prophecy will fall into different categories

I now want to 'categorise' prophetic words under four headings. These four headings are ones which I have borrowed from the teaching of Dale Gentry. It is of course possible to categorise them in other ways, but it seems that these four headings are the probably the easiest and best for us to work with.

A prophetic word will normally be categorised under one of these four headings. This does not mean that a prophecy can only contain one category—it might in fact contain all four distinct categories.

The category headings are:

i) A now word

This simply means that the prophecy is speaking to a current situation. If it was to an individual, then it would be speaking of this phase of their life. Many times there might be references to past events because such events often affect a person's life and their perception of God in the present.

ii) A future word

This is where the prophecy is speaking of things that will take place in the future. A future word is not given so that we can have our curiosity fulfilled regarding the future, but God speaks in this way to help us prepare for what lies ahead. Sometimes the prophecy might be referring to future events even if the tenses used were not future tenses. This can happen when the person speaking has not seen the situation totally accurately, or many times this occurs because God does not share our limited perspective on the future. To God a thousand years is as one day, and He wants us to believe His word concerning the future in the same way as He does. The fulfilment might still be future but the outcome is certain.

iii) A confirmatory word

There is a scriptural principle that facts need to be confirmed through the mouth of two or three witnesses (Deut. 19:15; Matt. 18:16). This would seem to be a pattern of the way that God speaks.

So many times a prophetic word will come which will give clear confirmation regarding a situation, an issue or a choice that is being made. This confirmatory word does not necessarily confirm previous prophetic words—it might simply be confirming something which is currently being experienced.

iv) New words.
God can come and speak words to us which are entirely new. They are words which have not previously been entertained in our thoughts. If this occurs we simply need to wait and allow God, in His own way, to confirm that the new words are from Him. We would be foolish to adjust the whole course of our life immediately around one new word. Rather we should wait and allow God to confirm the reality of this new word. It is our responsibility to test everything. This confirmation might not come through further prophetic words, but will often come through fellowship and the counsel of those we submit to.

4. Record the word, meditate on it and pray over it (1 Tim. 1:18)

If it is at all possible to have the prophecy recorded on tape then I advise that to be done. Once it is recorded it can then be transcribed. This makes it much easier to weigh it in detail, to meditate and pray over it—and also to remember it!

Keeping a record of the word will be a great encourage-ment when any doubts arise as to whether God has spoken or not. It is also very encouraging to see God fulfil His word—if we have a record of it then it is easy to monitor this fulfilment.

The fulfilment of prophecy is not automatic and, as Paul wrote to Timothy, there are times we will need to get hold of the words that God has given us and begin to make war with them through prayer. We will need to pray the will of God, as revealed in the prophecies, into existence.

By recording the prophecy we will also be able to open it up for others to make comment on it—which is the next principle we will look at.

5. Open it up for fellowship and interpretation

Prophecy should not be a matter for private interpretation, and it is vital that we invite comments from others on prophetic words which we have received. This is particularly true of the comments of those who are mature and have a shepherding role in our life.

If we are locked up to our own perspectives we might find that we are unable to interpret the prophecy accurately. We all often fail to see how certain events in our own life can relate to God and His word—that is where we need other people.

With regard to prophecy there are times when the opposite to what was prophesied seems to begin to take effect. For instance, a person might receive a word that lets them know that God is about to lead them in an overcoming and victorious way. They begin to prepare themselves for this time of great blessing but immediately face trials and tribulations. If they are left to themselves they might begin to despair. They might even begin to question the validity of the prophecy. It is at such times they need the advice of others around them, who can help point out to them that the prophecy was an encouragement to them—it was speaking of God bringing them through these current difficulties. In fact the difficulties are giving the person the opportunity to overcome, and the prophecy is the encouragement that they need to continue to persevere because God is with them.

Many times we need help in interpreting prophecies because of our own preconceived ideas. For example, if a person received a prophecy concerning an evangelistic anointing being on them they might interpret the outworking of this word to mean that they will exercise a Billy Graham-type ministry. This might be the case if their only concept of evangelism was that of public preaching.

However perhaps the person has no real gifting in the public arena, but is able to befriend people very easily. To pursue an avenue of looking for public opportunities to open up would be fruitless and misleading. On the other hand, if they had opened this word up to their mature friends, those friends might well have explained how they could see this prophecy being fulfilled very easily. They would explain that the word was not to do with preaching, but in fact was a great encouragement for this person to believe that God was anointing them where they were—in their ability to make friends and subsequently to share the Gospel with them.

Another area where the recipient of a prophecy often needs help is with regard to the timing of its fulfilment. Even if there seemed to be an immediacy when the word was given, there is often a time gap between the giving, of the prophecy and the fulfilment. The prophetic word would need to be put in the context of all that God is doing in that person's life—so they could move forward step by step towards the fulfilment. Again this is where trusted friends and leaders are so helpful.

6. Make preparation for it at the appropriate time

Alongside the above phrase we also need to emphasise that we are not here to outwork prophecy. This is not an easy balance to get right. We must prepare ourselves to fulfil God's word, but our role is not to actively outwork His word and make sure it happens.

God must be the initiator; however, we are not to be passive. Our place is to co-operate with God. With all words there is a timing for their fulfilment, and if we are going to be ready we will need to prepare ourselves. It is spiritually true that the future belongs to those who pre-pare for it. Like the people of Israel we are to prepare ourselves today 'for tomorrow the Lord will do amazing things' (Joshua 3:5). We might not know when 'tomorrow' will take place, but we can prepare ourselves 'today'. Often the fulfilment takes a long time to begin to take place, but when it does begin it often takes place very rapidly. This is why preparing ourselves is vital.

This is perhaps best illustrated by giving an example. If God spoke prophetically to someone about their future ministry being in a certain country, then the wrong response for that person would be to try and open as many doors as possible into that country. God is the one who must open the door. However, there would come a time when that person would need to get acquainted with the culture and perhaps even learn the language of that country. That would be making preparations for the fulfilment. During this time, as they prayed over God giving them a connection in that nation, they should be actively waiting for God to open the door. When the door finally opened it would have been God who outworked the prophecy but it was they who prepared themselves. They were ready to go through the door that God had opened.

So in order to see prophecy fulfilled we need to co-operate with God. We do our part through preparing ourselves and we allow God to do His part. If He does not open the door of opportunity then we do not take it on ourselves to fulfil God's word. If He has spoken then our response is one of faith, for the promise is as good as the fulfilment. The Hebrew writer informs us that faith is the substance of what we hope for. As God speaks, our part is to believe that this is His word and subsequently as we wait on Him we take hold of this word and confess it back to God until He fulfils it. Only He can fulfil His word but we have our part to play.

If we apply the above principles to receiving prophecy then I believe we will find that prophecy really does come to encourage and equip us to fulfil His call in our lives.

CHAPTER 6

PROPHETS AND PROPHECY

With prophecy there are certain extreme positions we can take. On the one hand there is the approach which makes it a specialist and exclusive field only open to a few who are 'prophets'. This leaves the 'spirituals' as a mystery which was certainly not Paul's desire (1 Cor. 12:1). The opposite approach is to open it all up and devalue the prophetic realm by giving a platform to every spontaneous thought or picture and calling them prophetic. This will lead to the situation Paul spoke against in Thessalonica, where they were in danger of despising prophecy (1 Thess. 5:20).

We need to see the area of prophecy abounding. It needs to be opened up for all to participate in. Alongside this we need to see the development and release of prophets who will bring words which will go beyond the normal realm of prophecy.

It would seem to me that as the church matures we ought to expect an increase of prophetic ministry within the body. If prophetic ministry increases then the need for good biblical teaching on prophecy will be very important in order that people are taught how to discern the true from the false. If true prophets rise up then there will also be the greater possibility of some false prophets also appearing. These false prophets will cause destruction. If there is a lack of discernment confusion will result.

One possible answer is to play safe by reacting with fear and stifling the prophetic. However, the best response is to raise the level of discernment. By raising the discernment level we will be able to clearly receive the benefits of those who bring the prophetic word to us.

Discernment is necessary because it is very easy to judge something by its methodology. Prophets cannot be judged simply on the basis of how they prophesy. Providing the method used is not forbidden in Scripture, we need to allow room for differences of approach. Even a cursory reading of the Old Testament prophets will clearly illustrate the tremendous divergence of personality and ministry that God used. Jesus taught us to judge something by the fruit that it bore, and this must be the ultimate test of all prophetic ministry (Matt. 7:16). True prophetic ministry will always point to and exalt Jesus, as the spirit of prophecy bears witness to Him (Rev. 1 9:10).

If we do not raise the discernment level then we could end up with whole churches being led astray because of naivety, where they are convinced something is of God simply because of its accuracy. So there is a great need to ground people in clear biblical teaching and in healthy submission to leadership. This submission to leadership is not in order to exercise control but to guide and protect the church.

I now want to address the issue of prophets and prophecy with some thoughts on the prophetic office as one of the key ministries God will use to bring the church to maturity (Eph. 4:11-16).

1. Inspiration and revelation

Prophecy is often in the realm of inspiration. When there is a release of the prophetic spirit everyone may prophesy through the inspiration of the Spirit. At such times it seems that everyone can be inspired to say something which comes from God. However, if in a meeting context everyone was to release their inspired words, it would eventually become too much for people to receive. Rather than enhance prophecy it would in fact devalue it. The consequence would be that respect for prophecy would eventually decrease. This would seem to be the case at Corinth, where Paul restricts the giving of prophecy to two or three prophetic words, and again was probably the problem at

Thessalonica where they were in danger of despising prophecy (1 Cor. 14:29; 1 Thess. 5:20).

Prophets, on the other hand, don't simply move under the inspiration of the Spirit, but often speak out of revelation they have received. They do not have to wait for the inspiration of the Holy Spirit, in a specific context, but speak and act from what has been shown to them by the Holy Spirit. This revelation is something which they have been seeing for some time and can often be in the form of a progressive revelation. Some of what has been shown to them will be for their own prayers, and they might not feel at liberty to share all they have seen or they might simply feel free to share it in a limited context.

This ability to see is fundamental to the prophetic office. The Old Testament affirms this when it states that such people who are known as prophets were originally called 'seers'. Many times God spoke to the prophets through visions. They often declared out what they had seen. God even asked a number of them to describe what they saw, (Jer. 1:11,13; Amos 7:8; 8:2 are examples of God asking this question to two prophets.)

On one occasion Jesus even asked an offended Pharisee if he could see a prostitute who had broken in on their meal! He asked him, 'Do you see this woman?' (Luke 7:44). Jesus was not 'questioning' Simon's physical eyesight but He was certainly making a comment on his ability to see from God's perspective. Ironically, a few minutes earlier Simon had clearly judged Jesus' prophetic ministry on the basis that He had not rebuked the woman (Luke 7:39). Through this incident Jesus clearly teaches that the one with true prophetic ministry sees at a deeper level—such a person sees something from God's viewpoint.

Isaiah claims that he saw the Lord seated on His throne (Isaiah 6:1). This was foundational to his prophetic ministry and should be the pattern for all subsequent prophetic ministry. True prophetic ministry is motivated by the prophet's vision of the Lord and His kingdom. For the prophet everything will be measured up against that.

These areas of revelation do not always come in strict picture form. They can come as a burden from God which the prophet will willingly (even if at times reluctantly) carry. They are fundamentally to do with the area of inner vision. It is that inner image which draws and motivates the prophet.

Many times it does come in vision form and it is worth noting that there are different types of visions. There is the simple *inner picture* which is painted on a person's spirit, mind or imagination. Then there is what is sometimes termed an *open vision* where the picture is as real and tangible as anything else in the physical realm. The vision is seen clearly with eyes opened or closed. There is also the realm of the *prophetic dream* which occurs during sleep. Finally there is the realm of the *trance*. In a trance a person's senses are temporarily placed in suspension during this powerful vision—it leaves the person not knowing whether they were in the body or not (2 Cor. 12:2). This was the level of vision Peter received while praying on the roof at Joppa (Acts 10:9–23). With the trance and the open vision there are times when a very powerful communication from God is heard, possibly sometimes even in the form of an audible voice.

2. A foundational ministry

The prophet can come to uproot, tear down, destroy, overthrow and also to build and plant (Jer. 1:10). Such radical ministry can have powerful and even devastating results, so it is understandable why the prophet needs to be particularly tied in with the apostle or an apostolic team (Ephes. 2:20).

Part of the tearing-down aspect of the prophetic ministry will mean that at times sin is uncovered. Other times a plumbline will be brought against a whole work, and areas which are out of order will be revealed. Such ministry might not be popular but is very much needed. However, prophetic ministry also builds up. Consequently prophetic ministry can come and unlock potential and gifting in people that has been dormant for years. Whether tearing down or building up it is essential that the prophet serves the local leadership and does not dictate direction. The ministry gifts are there to serve the body; local leadership is there to receive and release them.

3. Beyond the realm of prophecy

A prophet is not simply limited to the realm of edification, exhortation and comfort. Many times prophetic ministry will move beyond this. Regardless of the sphere a prophet is moving in his first role is to protect the people he is speaking to. A prophets overwhelming desire must be to protect the church as it is the bride of Christ.

At times the prophet comes in to bring correction but even that correction will only be given because of a desire to protect the church. The true mature prophet is motivated by a love for the Lord and His church. Alongside the correcting ministry there is also a directional ministry which a prophet brings. Through this direction confirmation is often brought. At times though, redirection and even new direction comes to a church or an individual through prophetic ministry. Prophets do not give such direction lightly nor to prove themselves to be superior. The motivation can only be because they want to extend the Lord's protection to this situation.

4. A divergence of ministry

There can be a tremendous difference in the way that prophets operate and we must not try and make them all fit the same mould. Their mode of operation and also the outworking of their ministry can be very different. For example, some will move more powerfully in the word of knowledge, others will excel at prophetic counselling, some will prophesy clearly regarding the future, others will have a ministry to individuals while others will prophesy to churches. These are simply a few examples of the great variety that is found among prophetic ministries. It would be wrong to make all prophetic ministries fit the same mould and we need to understand this if we are to gain from the variety that God places within His body.

Along the same lines it is equally true that prophets should not assume that because they move well in one sphere, they can move with equal authority in another sphere. This is seldom the case and prophets need to learn the sphere and boundaries that God has assigned for them. Of course their sphere might expand as they develop in God, but this simply highlights another area where relationships will prove to be the safeguard.

5. Churches need to be committed to see prophets released

If there are budding prophetic ministries within a church, then the leadership of that church needs to be committed to see those people developed. Those people will need protecting and encouraging. Many times the protection will be from themselves rather than from other people as they learn to live with God's anointing and burden. They will need to learn how to relax and enjoy life as well as carry the burden of the Lord. They will need encouraging as they seek to serve the church and particularly as they make mistakes while they are in the process of maturing.

Many people speak of the 'prophetic temperament' but this is not to become an excuse for sin and self-pity. Leadership needs to bring strong discipline in the area of character. Regardless of how gifted a person is, leadership must insist on a teachable humble spirit being present in the one who is called to function prophetically.

There are some common weaknesses which tend to surface in those called to prophetic ministry. Leadership must not pander to these weaknesses. Rejection will have to be dealt with or the prophet will eventually project this on to the listeners. It will actually become a self-fulfilling prophecy! The prophet will expect rejection and receive it. Isolation often clings to those with a rejection complex. This is very dangerous as it is the work of Satan to isolate us so that he can pick us off when we are vulnerable.

The other weaknesses often stem from pride. Such things as perfectionism, exclusiveness and superiority must be dealt with as they become a snare if left to develop.

Perhaps there is a 'prophetic temperament'. However, in all of this the character plumb line must be the Prophet who came to reveal the heart of the Father. It is for this reason that we compromise regarding character to our eventual downfall.

CHAPTER 7

PROPHETS AND OTHER MINISTRIES

Prophets are a key ministry and it is essential that the church receives prophetic ministry in order to reach maturity. Prophets are key but they are only *one* of the ministries which Christ sends to mature His body. No ministry—however gifted—can supply everything the church needs. The prophet is no exception to this.

The New Testament prophet is not some isolated individual who lives life in a secluded cave, then comes out to prophesy a devastating word and subsequently disappears back into the cave. The prophet is part of the body of Christ and as such needs to be involved within the network of relationships which make up the body of Christ.

A prophet will work alongside other ministries. There are certain specific ministries that the prophet is ideally suited to partner in ministry. These partnerships are given specific mention in the New Testament, and I believe there is particular significance in that. Obviously, as with all people, the prophet needs relationships both at a friendship, and a functional level, so I am not suggesting that the combination of ministries that are listed below are the only working relationships for the prophet—although as I have stated I believe there is a special importance with these particular partnerships for the prophet.

1. Prophets together

Acts 11:27 states that a number of prophets came down

from Jerusalem to Antioch. It would seem that they were travelling together as a prophetic team. One of the prophets on this team, named Agabus, stood up to give a very profound and important revelation. It is easy to assume that Agabus moved in a remarkable depth of prophetic ministry and that was how he gave this startling prediction. This might well be true of him; however, I believe the details shared, and the accuracy, had something to do with the fact that he was travelling in a prophetic team. The prophetic anointing was probably heightened, and as a result, so was the level of revelation.

Prophets working together will cause prophetic ministry to come through at a faster rate. As they work together the prophets will 'spark' one another and the prophetic anointing will be heightened in each other. This is an exciting situation and also challenging for in such settings competitiveness would be extremely destructive.

It is interesting to note that in the other mention of Agabus in Acts we find him in Caesarea, giving Paul a significant word regarding his future. Philip lived in Caesarea and had four daughters who prophesied (Acts 21:8–11). It is possible that Agabus spent time with those four daughters on occasions and encouraged them. If this was the case then we have another example of prophets meeting together and possibly working together. However, even if this was not the case in this situation I do not believe that the traditional view of Agabus as some wandering prophet is totally accurate. He seems to be a man who had some key relationships.

Another example from Acts of prophets working together is of Judas and Silas travelling together to minister on behalf of what is known as the Jerusalem Council. Acts 15:32 says that they encouraged and strengthened the churches because they were both prophets.

In the Old Testament there are a number of mentions of 'the school of the prophets'. These schools gave opportunity for budding prophets to learn from those who were more experienced. As they met together the prophets would have been a stimulus to each other, and it would seem that there is sufficient New Testament evidence to suggest that this is an area which could be further explored in church circles today, with some significant results.

2. Prophets and teachers

In Acts 13:1-3 we read of prophets and teachers meeting together. They were a significant group at Antioch and were the main group involved in deciding to release Paul and Barnabas to their apostolic call. We do not know if this group was the local leadership team at Antioch or not, but it seems significant that Luke was led to record the group as a collection of prophets and teachers.

Both the prophet and the teacher is consumed by God's word. However, their approach is different. For the prophet there is the challenge and burden of always moving forward and receiving new revelation from God. The teacher, however, wants the listeners to gain an understanding of what has been said. To the teacher nothing has been taught until it has been learned.

It is because of this difference between them that they need each other. Many times after the prophet has spoken prophetically, the teacher needs to break down the prophetic words and make them palatable. The prophet gives the word as a whole—it would be like handing a loaf of bread to someone to eat. The teacher comes and slices it up so that the 'loaf' can be eaten with ease. The teacher makes the word attainable. There are also times when the teacher will need the prophet either to open up the ground for a teaching word, or to follow up a teaching word with prophetic application.

There can be tensions between the two approaches to God's word, but it is important that the prophet and the teacher gain a respect for each other so that they can effectively work together and the church be the beneficiary.

3. Prophets and apostles

Paul states clearly in Ephesians 2:20 that these two ministries working together are essential for good foundations. It is easy to see how this is necessary as these two ministries clearly complement each other. The prophet can help see the areas that need attention, but it is the apostle who has the wisdom of how to put this in place and implement it. The prophet might see the final product, but the apostle is gifted as the wise master builder (1 Cor. 3:10). It is the apostle who will know how to move the church forward one step at a time towards the goal.

From 1 Corinthians 12:28 it would appear that the above three ministries—the apostle, the prophet and the teacher—are essential ingredients in the growth and maturity of the church. Teams which consist of those ministries are very important. (Obviously alongside these three ministries are the other ministry gifts in Eph. 4:11.)

If prophets simply work alone there is the very real danger that they will go off on a tangent through a lack of checks and balances. The other and opposite problem that can arise for prophets who work alone is that they feel obliged to try and balance out their own ministry by trying to fulfil other ministry roles. This will blunt their prophetic edge and they will be functioning in areas where they have not been anointed.

This current chapter is simply designed to stimulate thought over exploring ways that prophets need to work with others. It is not intended to be an exhaustive study. Regardless of how the ideas presented are outworked, we do need to recognise the danger of any ministry working alone. On this matter God's word has always been and still is 'team'.

CHAPTER 8

PROPHETIC MINISTRY AND LEADERSHIP

Prophetic ministry in the local church needs to be tied into leadership. The normal place for a prophet to develop is within the local church under the local oversight. There is also clearly a place for the prophet to function as a travelling ministry—normally as part of an apostolic team. When ministering in a local church the prophet would submit himself to the oversight of that church.

The interrelationship of the prophetic ministry to leadership is one which needs to be spelt out clearly, otherwise tension or intimidation can arise. Tension will come in through misunderstanding while intimidation can arise through insecurity. These tensions and insecurities can be present on either side.

If we realise that the prophetic office and that of oversight are involved in two distinct spheres, then it will help us to bring definition to their interrelationship. Overseeres are responsible for the shepherding of the local church. This means that, along with other responsibilities, they take responsibility for who they allow to minister to their flock (Acts 20: 28–31). They should be prepared to close the door to ministries that they do not believe will further God's will among the people given to them to care for. They need also to be prepared to open up the church to ministries that will bless the people with God's word, even if the result is that their own work load is increased.

There are some overseers who close the door to prophets because they take the attitude of 'we have enough problems already without also having the word of God to come to terms with!' God wants to build strong churches with clear, confident overseers who are keen to welcome His word. Such overseers will want to have the prophetic word of God proclaimed among them, even if the outworking of those words mean change.

The responsibility of overseers is for the flock under their care—the responsibility of the prophet is to release the word of God.The prophet is not responsible for the outworking of that word. It is the overseers who bear the responsibility of weighing the word and making the necessary adjustments in the light of it. Their spheres of responsibility therefore differ.

In a local church the prophets need to be waiting on the Lord so that they are open to hear Him speak. They then need to release that word through the oversseers who in turn need to seek God, how to administer the prophetic revelation. To facilitate this I think it is often a good idea to have the overseers meeting with prophets from time to time so that together they can wait on the Lord.

Some prophets also carry an anointing to be part of the oversight. However, many prophets cannot carry this extra burden, and to place that on their shoulders would only blunt their ministry. If these prophets were also to live with the outworking of their word they might soon stop receiving revelation! So leadership needs to be sensitive about placing demands on people that they are not equipped to fulfil.

On the other hand, in some churches prophets are excluded from spending quality time on oversight simply because they themselves are not overseers. Churches need strong overseers who welcome the word of God from all— but particularly from those who have prophetic ministries.

Prophets need access to leadership and leadership needs to be open to prophetic ministry. They need each other. Prophets are needed in the church but prophetic ministry must never be exalted to the place where the church is governed by those with prophetic anointing (unless they also serve as overseers). The government and responsibility for the church lies with the overseers (who ideally are in partnership with apostolic ministry).

Another responsibility that leaders carry is to ensure that the church is adequately taught and equipped. It is their responsibility to ensure that the people under their care are mature enough to handle prophetic ministry. The challenge before leaders is not to sit back and decide from a distance what they make of certain prophetic people or practices, but actively to consider how they are going to train their people to handle prophetic ministry.

God does not want us to compromise at any level—the task before us of reaching this generation with the Gospel is great, and we shall need to see every person standing in their right place if we are to see God move with victory through His church. To bring this about He is looking for a strong church: a church where leaders lead fearlessly; a church where the gifts of the Spirit are in evidence; a church where all the ministries are being released—including the prophets; and a church where there is a maturity to weigh and receive prophecy—and prophets. This will only happen as leaders begin to move forward clearly, without fear and open to all that the Holy Spirit is seeking to do. The challenge is for leadership to open the door to the Holy Spirit and all He wants to do, regardless of how demanding that might be.